Biu Jee (Darting Fingers)

Wing Chun

Brutality

of

Biu Jee

Lavishly illustrated throughout, demonstrated and written by

Sifu Mark Beardsell

Lifetime member of: Ving Tsun Athletic Assoc- H K.
International Wing Chun Martial Art Assoc.
World Ving Tsun Athletic Assoc.

Instructor- Samuel Kwok Martial Arts Assoc.
Instructor- World Ving Tsun Athletic Assoc.
Red Sash- International Wing Chun Martial Art Assoc.

Copyright Mark Beardsell 2014

Biu Jee (Darting Fingers)

Contents

Dedication	Page 4
Preface	Page 5
Ip Man Code of Conduct	Page 7
Chapter 1 - History	Page 9
Translation of Biu Jee sometimes called Biu Tze	Page 11
Chapter 2 – Starting the form	Page 13
Chapter 3 - Biu Jee - Section 1 (Kup Jaan)	Page 17
Huen Ma - Circling step	Page 20
Kup Jaan Usage 1	Page 24
Kup Jaan Usage 2 - juk cheung	Page 25
Kup Jaan Usage 2 - dai cheung	Page 27
Chapter 4 - Biu Jee - Section 2	Page 29
High/Low Gaan Sau	Page 29
Fak Sau and Huen Sau	Page 30
Biu jee sau (lin wan biu jee)	Page 31
Chapter 5 - Biu Jee - Section 3	Page 32
Double lap sau	Page 32
Sheung lo man sau	Page 33
Chapter 6 - Biu Jee - New Techniques	Page 35
Kup Jaan	Page 35
Two way energy with Effective Yiu Ma	Page 36
Huen Ma - Circling Step	Page 36
Under hand biu jee sau	Page 37
Double Lap Sau	Page 37
Sheung Lo Man Sau	Page 38
Chapter 7 - Biu Jee - Chi Sau	Page 39
Chapter 8 - Biu Jee - The Full form	Page 42

Biu Jee (Darting Fingers)

Biu Jee (Darting Fingers)

Dedication

This book is dedicated to all those past and present who have guided me on my Wing Chun journey and without whose knowledge, guidance and patience it would not be possible to pass on this gift to help those on similar paths to achieve their goals, this book is my way of thanking you all.

A big thanks to my father for his thirst for knowledge of martial arts and dragging me to classes which without I would not have been able to write this book.

I would also like to thank my Sifu Grandmaster Samuel Kwok for taking me under his wing and for passing on the Wing Chun of Ip Man in accordance with his wishes so that it will not be forgotten, which I, in turn will pass on to as many people as I can.

Biu Jee (Darting Fingers)

Preface

Before reading this book you should have read the Siu Lim Tau and the Chum Kiu book as trying to attempt what is found in this book will just be very poor to the onlooker and to the receiver that you are in an encounter with.

I spent a great deal of time researching the Biu Jee from as the other two forms are well documented however this form is not, they are even broken down into three section and are clearly defined but I found no such documentation to indicate where the breaks are in this form, if you were to ask someone this form would be shrouded in mystery stating that this form was only taught to a special few and behind close doors, the actual truth of this is there is not video proof of the form being performed as they say that Ip Man was too weak due to his illness to film this.

In an attempt to formalize it and break it down into logical parts that you can understand, this book has my take on how the form should be logically laid out.

This is what I perceive section one of the form should be

The form starts as normal with a slight change where you enact a powerful lap action, after which you demonstrate a powerful punch followed by vertical and horizontal jut sau's first on the left and then on the right hand side.

Then, starting with the left hand three kup jaan's (downward striking elbow) are done first to the right of the body, then to the left and back to the right, this is followed by a biu jee then with a step and another biu jee, using the huen ma stepping to bring you to forward facing again this is then performed on the opposite side.

Biu Jee (Darting Fingers)

After a repeat of what you did is performed, followed by another possible way to use the kup Jaan and taking you to a juk cheung (side strike) enacted on both sides and then the same thing is done but this time it a rib cage strike take place and this called dai cheung (low palm strik).

I believe that the first part teaches you kup Jaan and then the second part of the form teaches you how to use the kup Jaan and then three varied responses/uses that accompany the kup Jaan.

This for me is the end of section 1 and the start of section two. I believe that these next actions performed, are for multiple attackers in given emergency situations, at multiple angles, we see double gaan sau used first left, then right, then left again. Next you see three fak sau's and three huen sau's and these are also repeated on the opposite side of the body, then to complete (what I consider to be the middle section by logically examining the techniques used is three biu jee strikes) that go under each other, then there are strikes performed to each side of you via a juk cheung and then behind you a fak sau, again you see the pattern of multiple attackers.

Its here that I break off and call this last section the emergency recovery technique, when there is no other way to defend yourself, the first is a double lap sau,... why? There is so much power coming at you, you need two hands to control it and respond to it, next imagine you have fallen to the ground, or have been pushed to the ground, here we see a technique to help recover from that, resulting in a true emergency recovery to get you fighting again, this leading on to 5 chain punches to end. So if you read and learn from this book keep in mind what have said here.

Biu Jee (Darting Fingers)

Ip Man Code of Conduct

守 紀 律 崇 尚 武 德

Remain disciplined - uphold yourself ethically as a martial artist

明 禮 義 愛 國 尊 親

Practice courtesy and righteousness - serve the community and honour your family

愛 同 學 團 結 樂 群

Love your fellow students or classmates - be united and avoid conflicts

節 色 慾 保 守 精 神

Limit your desires and pursuit of bodily pleasures - preserve the proper spirit

勤 練 習 技 不 離 身

Train diligently and make it a habit - maintain your skills

學 養 氣 救 濫 鬥 民

Learn to develop spiritual tranquillity - abstain from arguments and fights

Biu Jee (Darting Fingers)

常 處 世 態 度 溫 民

Participate in society - be conservative, cultured and gentle in your manners

扶 弱 小 以 武 輔 仁

Help the weak and the very young - use your martial skill for the good of humanity

繼 光 緒 漢 持 祖 訓

Pass on the tradition - preserve this Chinese art and its rules of conduct

Biu Jee (Darting Fingers)

Chapter 1 – History

I always like to include the history of where are art comes from and I feel we should always honour the people that gave us what we are left with today.

In the late 1600's and early 1700's Kung Fu became very popular at the Siu Lam (Shaolin) monastery in Honan Province, Siu Lam or Shaolin translates to " little trees", The Kung Fu exercises were designed to help keep the monks and abbots awake during long periods of mental training and meditation. By exercising their bodies as well as their minds they developed even further in their spiritual training. The Manchu (non-Chinese) government in the North at the time were deeply suspicious of such activities, believing the monastery to be training an army. They eventually attacked the monastery, burning it to the ground and killing many of the monks and disciples. A few escaped the attack though, and they are thought to have been the Buddhist nun Ng Mui, Abbot Chi Shin, Abbot Pak Mei, Fung To Tak and Master Miu Hin.

So Wing Chun was first heard of around 300 to 400 years ago when the Shaolin nun who had escaped the temple, first introduced this style to a young woman, the daughter of a bean curd trader by the name of Yim Yee, she was being persued by a suitor who wanted to marry her, but she was not interested, and was trying to dissuade him. Ng Mui seeing her plight approached her and offered to teach her this new style to defend herself against the suitor, this style worked well because of a woman's physical frame being smaller than that of a man and worked well for fighting and also the pigeon toed footwork suited the bound feet of the Chinese women of the time too.

Biu Jee (Darting Fingers)

Like all kung fu styles, this style was based on the movements of animals in this case the snake and crane. It is said that Ng Mui spent many hours observing the movements of these creatures leading up to developing this new style of kung fu.

The original snake and crane style had only the Siu Lim Tau and the Bart Cham Dao as that was all that was needed at that time. Needless to say that Yim Wing Chun went on to beat the suitor and he left her alone after that. Yim Wing Chun sometime in the future went on to marry a man by the name of Leung Bok Chau who was an accomplished martial artist, but on seeing this new style that was taught to his wife, asked her to teach him, this she did and later on her husband named the style Wing Chun after his wife.

Leung Bok Chau went on to pass Wing Chun on to a man by the name of Leung Lan Kwai, who in turn passed it on to Wong Wah Bo then to Leung Yee Tai, it was at this time that Leung Yee Tai met Abbot Chi Shin hiding away as a cook with the Red opera and Chi Shin taught the pole to Leung Yee Tai, some time later Leung Yee Tai met Wong Wah Bo who passed Wing Chun on to Leung Yee Tai in exchange for teaching him the pole, and so the Lik dim boon kwan (*six and a half point long pole*) was added to the system.

It was at this time that Leung Yee Tai passed Wing Chun on to a young man by the name of Leung Jan, he is known for adding clarity and definition to the Wing Chun system, by that I mean he became the most accomplished student of Wing Chun and went about writing down the system for future students to learn from. It's about this time that we become aware of the addition of the Mok Yan Jong (Wooden Man) the Chum Kiu form (bridge seeking/sinking) and the emergency techniques for the advanced student known as the Biu Jee. Leung Jan went on to teach many his system but most notably was Chan Wah Shun and his elder son

Biu Jee (Darting Fingers)

Leung Bik. This is where things really start to get familiar, Wing Chun was then taught to many in Foshan/Fatsan but the one name that is popular around the world today is Ip Man aka Yip Man, a name made famous by the exploits of our all time favourite martial artist Bruce Lee, through him we see the first Wing Chun taught to Non-Chinese in America.

Ip Man first learned Wing Chun under Chan Wah Shun also know as Chan the money changer as that was his profession, Chan Wah Shun died before completing Ip Man's Wing Chun training and so his training was finished by his Si-hing, after the Japanese invasion of China, Ip Man escaped to Hong Kong and began openly teaching Wing Chun there, it was here that he met Leung Jan's son Leung Bik, it is said that the young, very sure of himself Ip man could not be beaten and when given the chance to fight with this man, Ip man was beaten by him and went away a little disgruntled, later he was to learn on a second encounter with this man that he was Leung Bik, and with that Ip Man became his student, Chan Wah Shun was quite a bulky person so his Wing Chun came across very heavy, however the Wing Chun of Leung Bik was soft and this is what allowed Leung Bik to overcome Ip Man. Sadly Ip Man passed away in 1972 but his two sons Ip Chun and Ip Ching continue to pass Wing Chun around the world most notably today is Samuel Kwok who works very hard in promoting Wing Chun world wide.

Translation of Biu Jee sometimes called Biu Tze

What does biu jee translate as, well they are Cantonese words of course being a southern Chinese martial art, biu means to move fast or dart and jee is the Cantonese word for fingers so this form translates as **darting fingers**.

IMPORTANT NOTICE

Again I cannot stress this enough, if you do not have a clear understanding to Siu Lim Tau and Chum Kiu this book will not work for you, the best analogy is like building a roof on a house where you have not built the foundation or walls it is that simple, this is not a rouse to get you to learn the first two books first, you really do need to know that stuff.

Biu Jee (Darting Fingers)

Chapter 2 - Starting the form

In the previous forms you learned how to do a crossed hand double gaan sau followed by a crossed had double tan sau.

In this form it is done differently, you start off with the crossed hand double gaan sau and then from that position then point the fingertips towards the stomach and continue to circle round until your hands reach a crossed double tan sau and then without a moment's pause withdraw them to sout kuen / hau Jaan.

Biu Jee (Darting Fingers)

Starting with the left hand as usual, next comes a punch to the chin through the centerline, but this time it differs to that of the first two forms, as you bring your fist to the center of your chest, do not pause, but fire that punch out full power.

Keeping your hand out there, unclench your fist and bend your hand with the fingers pointing up and the wrist pushed down, this is a jut sau, without a pause, point your tensed fingers downward keeping the arm locked out making the wrist come up. Repeat this action another two times enacting this sequence a total of three times.

After the third one turn your hand horizontally with your palm pointing down and push the side of your hand off to the left and your fingers off to the right, this is a sideways jut sau, without a pause push your fingers in the other direction forcing your wrist of

Biu Jee (Darting Fingers)

the right, your fingers should not be pointing to the left, again repeat this action another two times.

On completion of the third one withdraw your arm to sout kuen / how Jaan.

With the right hand, next comes a punch to the chin through the centerline, just like the other hand it differs to that of the first two forms, as you bring your fist to the center of your chest, do not pause but fire that punch out at full power.

Keeping your hand out there, unclench your fist and bend your hand with the fingers pointing up and the wrist pushed down, this is a jut sau, without a pause, point your tensed fingers downward keeping the arm locked out making the wrist come up. Repeat this action another two times enacting this sequence a total of three times.

Biu Jee (Darting Fingers)

After the third one turn your hand horizontally with your palm pointing down and push the side of your hand off to the right and your fingers off to the left, this is a sideways just sau, without a pause push your fingers in the other direction forcing your wrist of the left, your fingers should not be pointing to the right, again repeat this action another two times.

On completion of the third one withdraw your arm to sout kuen / how Jaan.

Biu Jee (Darting Fingers)

Chapter 3 - Biu Jee - Section 1 (Kup Jaan)

Let's first look at how to perform a correct kup Jaan or downward striking elbow.

Starting with your left hand, keep raising your hand, palm facing forward, until the side of your thumb knuckle is opposite your ear, but not touching your ear, twisting your hand so that you can see the back of your hand, keep your hand travelling down to meet your chest at the same time rotate your elbow through a high arc finally halting when your elbow is horizontal to the body in front of you and the back of your hand is resting on your chest, your back should be straight you should not be leaning forward or backwards.

I suggest you practice this a while on both side until it feel natural.

Now! On to the next part of the form.

So starting this part of the form, perform as explained above, using the a left hand kup jaan while turning from Siu Lim Tau ma to 90 degrees to the right with the weight on the rear leg, maintaining your waist at 45 degrees and also both of your feet at 45 degrees.

Then perform a right hand kup jaan while turning 180 degrees to the left and with the weight on the rear leg, maintaining your waist at 45 degrees and also both of your feet at 45 degrees and withdrawing your left hand to sout kuen.

Then perform a left hand kup jaan while turning 180 degrees to the right and with the weight on the rear leg, maintaining your waist at 45 degrees and also both of your feet at 45 degrees and this time place your right hand, palm down, fingers forward under your left elbow which is currently in kup jaan.

Biu Jee (Darting Fingers)

Biu Jee (Darting Fingers)

Biu Jee (Darting Fingers)

Biu Jee Sau

Strike out with your right biu jee sau, simultaneously modify your left hand from kup jaan to a rear biu see sau ready to fire.

Bring the back leg forward to meet your front leg, bringing your feet together at the same time fire your rear biu jee sau forward to meet your other hand, so both feet are together and both hands are together i.e. parallel biu jee sau's.

Huen Ma

Lift your heel on the left and sweep your left foot outward through an arc until your foot reaches the position where your left foot would be in Siu Lim Tau ma, lift the heel of the right foot and circle the right foot backwards to the left foot and outward in an arc until it reaches the position where the right foot would be in Siu Lim Tau ma, you should end up again in Siu Lim Tau ma.

Using the a right hand kup jaan while turning from Siu Lim Tau ma to 90 degrees to the left with the weight on the rear leg, maintaining your waist at 45 degrees and also both of your feet at 45 degrees.

Then perform a left hand kup jaan while turning 180 degrees to the right and with the weight on the rear leg, maintaining your waist at 45 degrees and also both of your feet at 45 degrees and withdrawing your right hand to sout kuen.

Then perform a right hand kup jaan while turning 180 degrees to the left and with the weight on the rear leg, maintaining your waist at 45 degrees and also both of your feet at 45 degrees and this time

Biu Jee (Darting Fingers)

place your left hand, palm down, fingers forward under your right elbow which is currently in kup jaan.

Biu Jee Sau

Strike out with your left biu jee sau, simultaneously modify your right hand from kup jaan to a rear biu see sau ready to fire.

Bring the back leg forward to meet your front leg, bringing your feet together at the same time fire your rear biu jee sau forward to meet you other hand, so both feet are together and both hands are together i.e. parallel biu jee sau's.

Huen Ma (Circling step)

Biu Jee (Darting Fingers)

Biu Jee (Darting Fingers)

Biu Jee (Darting Fingers)

Huen Ma

Lift your heel on the right and sweep your right foot outward through an arc until your foot reaches the position where your right foot would be in Siu Lim Tau ma, lift the heel of the left foot and circle the left foot backwards toward the right foot and outward in an arc until it reaches the position where the left foot would be in Siu Lim Tau ma, you should end up again in Siu Lim Tau ma.

Kup Jaan Usage 1

Using a left hand kup jaan while turning from Siu Lim Tau ma to 90 degrees to the right with the weight on the rear leg, maintaining your waist at 45 degrees and also both of your feet at 45 degrees, this time place your right hand, palm down, fingers forward under your left elbow which is currently in kup jaan. Strike out with your right biu jee sau, simultaneously modify your left hand from kup jaan to a rear biu see sau ready to fire.

Bring the back leg forward to meet your front leg, bringing your feet together, at the same time fire your rear biu jee sau forward to meet your other hand, so both feet are together and both hands are together i.e. parallel biu jee sau's. Now perform huen ma as demonstrated earlier.

Using a right hand kup jaan while turning from Siu Lim Tau ma to 90 degrees to the left with the weight on the rear leg, maintaining your waist at 45 degrees and also both of your feet at 45 degrees, this time place your left hand, palm down, fingers forward under your right elbow which is currently in kup jaan.

Strike out with your left biu jee sau, simultaneously modify your right hand from kup jaan to a rear biu see sau ready to fire.

Biu Jee (Darting Fingers)

Bring the back leg forward to meet your front leg, bringing your feet together at the same time fire your rear biu jee sau forward to meet you other hand, so both feet are together and both hands are together i.e. parallel biu jee sau's. Again perform huen ma as demonstrated earlier.

Kup Jaan Usage 2 - juk cheung

Using a left hand kup jaan while turning from Siu Lim Tau ma to 90 degrees to the right with the weight on the rear leg, maintaining your waist at 45 degrees and also both of your feet at 45 degrees, place your right hand, palm down, fingers forward under your left elbow which is currently in kup jaan, strike out with your right biu jee sau, simultaneously modify your left hand from kup jaan to an open hand sout kuen, while withdrawing your right hand to sout kuen shoot out the other hand to **juk cheung**, turn your right foot back into Siu Lim Tau and using the same hand that is in **juk cheung** look off to the left and perform fak sau, after which bring the fak sau hand leading via the elbow to jum sau, then into toot sau wipe off and finish with huen sau to sout kuen.

Using a right hand kup jaan while turning from Siu Lim Tau ma to 90 degrees to the left with the weight on the rear leg, maintaining your waist at 45 degrees and also both of your feet at 45 degrees, place your left hand, palm down, fingers forward under your right elbow which is currently in kup jaan, strike out with your left biu jee sau, simultaneously modify your right hand from kup jaan to an open hand sout kuen, while withdrawing your left hand to sout kuen shoot out the other hand to **juk cheung**, turn your left foot back into Siu Lim Tau and using the same hand that is in **juk cheung** look off to the right and perform fak sau, after which bring the fak sau hand leading via the elbow to jum sau, then into toot sau wipe off and finish with huen sau to sout kuen.

Biu Jee (Darting Fingers)

Biu Jee (Darting Fingers)

Kup Jaan Usage 3 - Dai cheung

Using a left hand kup jaan while turning from Siu Lim Tau ma to 90 degrees to the right with the weight on the rear leg, maintaining your waist at 45 degrees and also both of your feet at 45 degrees, place your right hand, palm down, fingers forward under your left elbow which is currently in kup jaan, strike out with your right biu jee sau, simultaneously modify your left hand from kup jaan to a to an open hand sout kuen, while withdrawing your right hand to sout kuen shoot out the other hand to **dai cheung**, turn your right foot back in to Siu Lim Tau and using the same hand that is in **dai cheung** look off to the left and perform fak sau, after which bring the fak sau hand leading via the elbow to jum sau, then into toot sau wipe off and finish with huen sau to sout kuen.

Using a right hand kup jaan while turning from Siu Lim Tau ma to 90 degrees to the left with the weight on the rear leg, maintaining your waist at 45 degrees and also both of your feet at 45 degrees, place your left hand, palm down, fingers forward under your right elbow which is currently in kup jaan, strike out with your left biu jee sau, simultaneously modify your right hand from kup jaan to a to an open hand sout kuen, while withdrawing your left hand to sout kuen shoot out the other hand to **dai cheung**, turn your left foot back in to Siu Lim Tau and and using the same hand that is in **dai cheung** look off to the right and perform fak sau, after which, bring the fak sau hand leading via the elbow to jum sau, then into toot sau wipe off and finish with huen sau to sout kuen.

Biu Jee (Darting Fingers)

Biu Jee (Darting Fingers)

Chapter 4 - Biu Jee - Section 2

I refer to this as the multiple attackers from multiple directions section of the form, as it is fairly obvious while enacting the section.

High/Low Gaan Sau (gao gaan dai gaan)

This section starts with high and low gaan sau's, the left hand is high on the first one and the right hand is low, so the first high/low gaan sau's travel from left to right, then right to left and back again, finally bring your right hand up to wu sau and then wipe away followed by huen sau.

Repeat that again, in the other direction, starting with the right high gaan sau and low left gaan sau, then switch in the other direction, and again switch, finally leading to the left hand in wu sau and so on.

Biu Jee (Darting Fingers)

Fak Sau and Huen Sau

Ok... don't forget we start with left hand, so this leads us on to three fak sau's with guarding a wu sau's, after the first fak sau you should move as quickly as you can without compromising form to enact a further two fak sau's... after the third bring the fak sau hand leading via the elbow to jum sau, pause and perform huen sau with cheun ma (turning step) the elbow during the cheun ma does not move the body travels through 45 degrees, then reset, bringing the hand to wu sau... pause and perform huen sau and turning step again, do this one more time after which move the arm into toot sau, wipe off and finish with huen sau to sout kuen.

This time we repeat this on the right hand, so again after the first fak sau you should move as quickly as you can without compromising form to enact a further two fak sau's... after the third bring the fak sau hand leading via the elbow to jum sau, pause and perform huen sau with cheun ma (turning step) the elbow during the cheun ma does not move the body travels through 45 degrees, bringing the hand to wu sau... pause and perform huen sau and turning step again, do this one more time after which move the arm into toot sau, wipe off and finish with huen sau to sout kuen.

Biu Jee (Darting Fingers)

Biu jee sau (lin wan biu jee)

Starting again with the left hand, shoot from sout kuen in to a reaching biu jee sau strike, the reaching adds power from the shoulder into the strike, travelling under the first strike perform one from the right hand withdrawing the left hand to a rear biu jee sau and repeat this again throwing the left hand forward and bring the right hand back to sout kuen, turn to the right 90 degrees and shoot the left leading hand in to juk cheung, return to Siu Lim Tau ma and fire off to the left with fak sau again leading via the elbow to jum sau, then into toot sau, wipe off and finish with huen sau to sout kuen.

This time on the right shoot from sout kuen in to a reaching biu jee sau strike, the reaching add power from the shoulder into the strike, travelling under the first strike perform one from the left withdrawing the right hand to a rear biu jee sau and repeat this again throwing the right hand forward and bring the left hand back to sout kuen, turn to the left 90 degrees and shoot the left leading hand in to juk cheung, return to Siu Lim Tau ma and fire off to the right with fak sau again leading via the elbow to jum sau, then into toot sau, wipe off and finish with huen sau to sout kuen.

Biu Jee (Darting Fingers)

Chapter 5 - Biu Jee - Section 3

In this very small section I refer to these techniques as truly emergency/recovery techniques as both parts can be use respond to a mistake or being caught on the hop and need something quickly to recover.

Double lap sau

In this his part of the form, both hands are placed out in front of you and are open, you then, after a small pause, close the hands and pull through and arc to the left as if you are pulling a person, if you did not pull downward, but pulled fairly horizontal, then punch under your leading arm, if you pulled down then punch over the leading arm, I will explain this further later. After the punch you perform a tok sau once, lock out the arm do huen sau and withdraw to sout kuen.

Biu Jee (Darting Fingers)

Now to repeat this on the right hand side, so both hands are placed out in front of you and are open, you then after a small pause, close the hands and pull through and arc to the right as if you are pulling a person, if you did not pull downward but pulled fairly horizontally, then punch under your leading arm, if you pulled down then punch over the leading arm. After the punch you perform a tok sau once, lock out the arm and do huen sau and withdraw to sout kuen.

Sheung lo man sau

Imagine if you will, for some reason you have ended up on the ground and being a wing chun fighter you REALY do, need to be on your feet, by putting your hands above your head (Sheung lo man sau) you are doing two things, firstly protecting your head and secondly putting out feelers on the way up to stick to your opponent to use your wing chun again.

Biu Jee (Darting Fingers)

To start this part of the form, stand with a left leading man sau and right wu sau, bend as far forward towards the ground as you can go, before starting the return journey back up throw both hands above your head, repeat this two more times.

Lin wan kuen

Enact chain punches, at least 5 times and finish.

End of the form.

Biu Jee (Darting Fingers)

Chapter 6 - Biu Jee - New Techniques

Kup Jaan

As you will know jaan is Cantonese for the elbow, but this is the first introduction of kup, meaning downward, so this translated to downward elbow.

The elbow should drive from the back and though an arc upwards and then downwards and finish horizontal in the front of the body, if you drop it too far then you will restrict your ability to fire off a biu jee sau, you can take a very high trajectory or medium high trajectory BUT it must be seen to come down over to be Kup Jaan as it could end up looking like gwoy jaan.

A common usage of kup jaan to biu sau is when someone pak sau's your elbow and you shoot the biu sau under arm to recover.

Another popular occurrence is found in chi sau where you push their right tan sau to their body then using kup jaan on your right you push their dip sau on top off the other hand you are pinning creating a trap then realizing your left hand and then punching.

In the form you see three ways of using the kup jaan in combat, the first is demonstrated as seen in the first part, but the next two are in close quarter combat for each the side, following up with a biu then depending on high or low strike a juk cheung or dai cheung.

Another use of the kup jaan is as a strike where you have lap'd someone and their head is low as seen on the front cover.

Biu Jee (Darting Fingers)

Two way energy with Effective Yiu Ma

As you progress with your biu jee training, you should focus not only with the hand that is striking, but the rear hand too, that is pulling, this is referred to as two way energy, when this is performed effectively, the waist energy is used well and the two action compliment each over. This can be seen in the kup jaan section, as you strike with the kup jaan the other hand should withdraw to sout kuen at the same speed, thus applying the rue of two way energy with effective yiu ma, another instance of this is during the underhand biu jee before turning to perform juk cheung as one hand biu's the other hand pulls. Again in the application section of kup jaan, just after the biu jee sau, treat the other hand, as a lap sau as the striking juk cheung or dai cheung comes forward.

Huen Ma - Circling step

This is the first time we see the circling step, you will apply this in the future when doing the dummy form (muk yan jong) basically regardless of the classic martial art, when the attacker is in an arrow stance, with the right front leg forward and planted, the idea is that you circle around the your right leg and break his grounding. If someone has a shallow stance and you try to use this step, then you must make contact with their body, circling around their leg with your heel high and while both legs are in contact slam down your heel and the person will go flying. You can of course just circle around their leg to avoid the obstacle, allowing you to attack with one of the many techniques found in the dummy form, but of course you are at the biu jee stage so you will have already started play with the dummy, after all it's part of the fun and fascination of the form.

Biu Jee (Darting Fingers)

Under hand biu jee sau

As mentioned before, within Siu Lim Tau and Chum Kiu most of your continuous hand attacks would be one hand over the other hand, in biu jee we now see the ability to attack under each hand, this is very useful in chi sau as it now gives you over hand and under hand techniques, which is great against people who only know Siu Lim Tau and Chum Kiu as they only know over hand so they don't see it coming, concepts like this define what Biu Jee is all about when it is referred to as the advanced form, and this is why 50 years ago it was only taught to a privileged few who proved themselves as a good person who had the ability to understand the purpose of biu jee, in those days it was taught behind closed doors so that the people learning Siu Lim Tau and Chum Kiu could not see what was going on. So thus the biu jee form became a bit of a mystery that everyone sought to learn.

Double Lap Sau

This is another emergency technique; imagine if you will, someone coming at you with a fast, powerful punch or even armed with a bladed weapon, you really don't want to be there when it arrives, using your turning (cheun ma) angle your body just like a matador and grab the forearm and elbow using both your hands and help the attacker along using there own force, if there is a pause as they pass, you maybe able to punch them or elbow them. i.e. If it's their right arm, then you should be positioned on the right side of them, as you turn, your left hand should make contact around the elbow area and the right hand should make contact with the wrist. You can use this option to deal with multiple attackers coming at you... But not all at once, just run!

Biu Jee (Darting Fingers)

Sheung Lo Man Sau

It roughly translates to English from Cantonese as "Two hands searching".

In some versions of the biu jee form you see some circling their arms backwards and then forwards, I don't do that, I bend forward heading for the ground and then both hands fly above the head before the head arrives to cover the head on the way up, this has two purposes firstly to cover the head on the way up recovering from a fall to the ground, wing chun people fight on their feet not on the ground secondly to regain some kind of contact while getting up, once a new contact is made you can fight like wing chun person again.

Biu Jee (Darting Fingers)

Chapter 7 - Biu Jee - Chi Sau

You could ask three separate people the same question

What is chi sau?

And you will get three different answers.

Here is my explanation, chi sau is a tool that you use in conjunction with one or more people on separate occasions to find as many possible scenarios where you are weak and get hit and then learn to not get hit by listening and responding to those attacks. Then when you have to take those skills into a fight for real, there is a good chance that you have the appropriate remove response needed to win. This is why you should explore other people martial arts, so there is a little surprise on that fearful day you have to fight for real.

After you have learned biu jee your chi sau will improve to another level, you should be able to deal with anyone who is chum kiu and down over to Siu Lim Tau, the reason for this is that in the biu jee form you learn how to use two-way energy much better and also learn how to strike from under arm as opposed to over arm which is seen in the first two forms.

As you may know there are some good old techniques you can use to open up the defense of your chi sau partner and get as few strikes , but you may have noticed that during your attack they got a hit in too. Yes, we have all been there.

I call this making holes in the fence rather than looking at the fence for the existing holes, the best way to look for holes rather than make them is to maintain a good defensive structure in your rolling, when you do tan sau make sure it is an affective tan sau and the

Biu Jee (Darting Fingers)

same with the bong, if its sloppy you will get hit a lot, this same rule applies to the other hand whether you're using Fook sau with elbow in or using a combination of pak sau and dip sau to control the arm. It is when your chi sau partner makes these fundamental mistakes that they leave themselves open.

At this stage of chi sau you should have better structure and be able to re-direct and maintain your position via Siu Lim Tau ma. This is achieved through correct positioning of the elbow.

And where do you learn this.... San bai fut... yes, that is right at the very start of wing chun in the Siu Lim Tau form called the "little idea". Through years of performing the first part of the form and using something called jaan dai lik is where you will build the strength in the elbow that is what changes your wing chun in leaps and bounds.

Another important element within chi sau is the use of energy; you should only use enough energy to keep a person at bay, what this means is when someone pushes you, only push back enough to stop them advancing on you, do not push back excessively to gain the upper hand, like a mentioned before look for holes in the fence and don't try to make your own. By reserving the amount of energy you are using you will be able to last much longer if not indefinitely. And take the opponent when the time is right.

The next thing to focus on is sensitivity, if you maintain your structure and stay soft (sun lik) you will be able to respond to the slightest of movements given off by your opponent's arms, when you flex your arm muscles, it slows down your ability to respond quickly, if you are a strong person you may feel the need to over-power your attacker this way, however this is not chi sau, its more like judo or wrestling. By not flexing and learning to use structure

Biu Jee (Darting Fingers)

through correct elbow position and weight distribution, you will be able to meet the average person's strength accordingly.

As previously mentioned armed with a handful of techniques you can smash through most people's defenses, but remember this is chi sau, its purpose is to teach you the right road to take so that when it comes down to the fight, what you learn during chi sau comes in to play, if you take into consideration everything that I have previously talked about then you will eventfully become technique-less.

Sometimes to gain the upper hand it pays to change position, by this I mean turn the body or step one way or the other, by doing so you can sometimes take the other person structure away from them and hit without obstruction. Utilizing the foot work from Chum Kiu and Biu Jee explore various ways of doing this.

When passing on your knowledge of chi sau the correct path to pass on is as follows:-

Sometimes you will see various pronunciations of the same word

Don Chi Sau or Dan Chi Sau (single sticking hand)

Lap sau or Lop sau (grab and pull)

Sheung Chi Sau (Two sticking hands)

Poon Sau (rolling hands)

Biu Jee (Darting Fingers)

Chapter 8 – Biu Jee - The Full form

Biu Jee (Darting Fingers)

Biu Jee (Darting Fingers)

Biu Jee (Darting Fingers)

Biu Jee (Darting Fingers)

Biu Jee (Darting Fingers)

Biu Jee (Darting Fingers)

Biu Jee (Darting Fingers)

Repeat this on the right hand side.

Biu Jee (Darting Fingers)

Kup jaan side one

Biu Jee (Darting Fingers)

Biu Jee (Darting Fingers)

Biu Jee (Darting Fingers)

Biu Jee (Darting Fingers)

Biu Jee (Darting Fingers)

Biu Jee (Darting Fingers)

Huen ma side one

Biu Jee (Darting Fingers)

Biu Jee (Darting Fingers)

Biu Jee (Darting Fingers)

Kup jaan side two

Biu Jee (Darting Fingers)

Biu Jee (Darting Fingers)

Biu Jee (Darting Fingers)

Biu Jee (Darting Fingers)

Biu Jee (Darting Fingers)

Huen ma side two

Biu Jee (Darting Fingers)

Biu Jee (Darting Fingers)

Biu Jee (Darting Fingers)

Kup jaan application section technique one

Biu Jee (Darting Fingers)

Biu Jee (Darting Fingers)

Biu Jee (Darting Fingers)

Biu Jee (Darting Fingers)

Biu Jee (Darting Fingers)

Biu Jee (Darting Fingers)

Biu Jee (Darting Fingers)

Biu Jee (Darting Fingers)

Biu Jee (Darting Fingers)

Biu Jee (Darting Fingers)

Biu Jee (Darting Fingers)

Biu Jee (Darting Fingers)

Kup jaan application section technique Two

Biu Jee (Darting Fingers)

Biu Jee (Darting Fingers)

Biu Jee (Darting Fingers)

Biu Jee (Darting Fingers)

Biu Jee (Darting Fingers)

Biu Jee (Darting Fingers)

Biu Jee (Darting Fingers)

Biu Jee (Darting Fingers)

Biu Jee (Darting Fingers)

Kup jaan application section technique Three

Biu Jee (Darting Fingers)

Biu Jee (Darting Fingers)

Biu Jee (Darting Fingers)

Biu Jee (Darting Fingers)

Biu Jee (Darting Fingers)

Biu Jee (Darting Fingers)

Biu Jee (Darting Fingers)

Biu Jee (Darting Fingers)

Biu Jee (Darting Fingers)

Double gaan sau onwards

Biu Jee (Darting Fingers)

Biu Jee (Darting Fingers)

Biu Jee (Darting Fingers)

Biu Jee (Darting Fingers)

Biu Jee (Darting Fingers)

Biu Jee (Darting Fingers)

Three fak sau's starting on left.

Biu Jee (Darting Fingers)

Three huen sau's section left side.

Biu Jee (Darting Fingers)

Biu Jee (Darting Fingers)

Biu Jee (Darting Fingers)

Repeat this sequence on the right from the start of fak sau.

Biu Jee (Darting Fingers)

Lin Wan Biu Jee Sau to juk cheung - left side

Biu Jee (Darting Fingers)

Biu Jee (Darting Fingers)

Biu Jee (Darting Fingers)

Again repeat this on the right hand side

Biu Jee (Darting Fingers)

Sheung gaan sau - left side

Biu Jee (Darting Fingers)

Biu Jee (Darting Fingers)

And again repeat this on the right hand side

Biu Jee (Darting Fingers)

Sheung lo man sau

Biu Jee (Darting Fingers)

Biu Jee (Darting Fingers)

Biu Jee (Darting Fingers)

Leading on to five punches

Biu Jee (Darting Fingers)

Biu Jee (Darting Fingers)

End of form

Biu Jee (Darting Fingers)

Currently I run a Wing Chun distance learning course via my website, and I also hold Wing Chun classes in the Stockton on Tees area, so please feel free to contact me if you are interested in lessons via mark@wingchun-ipman.com or call +44 (0) 7766 307432

Also, If you would like to get involved online then for further information and sign up of my Wing Chun distance learning course you can visit my website:-

http://www.wingchun-ipman.com

The course material remains the same however there are a a few variations of the course to suite each person's budget.

If you wish to you can connect with me via Facebook at:-

www.facebook.com/mbeardsell

www.ingramcontent.com/pod-product-compliance
Ingram Content Group UK Ltd.
Pitfield, Milton Keynes, MK11 3LW, UK
UKHW021411280525
6119UKWH00029B/444